F...
...
FOOD
RECIPES

Compiled by
Simon Haseltine

Illustrated with
bygone scenes by
A.R. Quinton

SALMON

Index

Title page: "The Ship Inn, Porlock, Somerset"

Printed and Published by Dorrigo, Manchester, England © Copyright

Piri Piri Chicken Skewers

**2 chicken breasts (cut into bite-size chunks)   1 lemon   1 red onion
2 tbsp. white wine vinegar   3 garlic cloves   2 tbsp. Worcestershire sauce
2 chilies   Handful fresh coriander   1 tbsp. sweet smoked paprika
Olive oil   4 wooden skewers (soaked in water for 30 minutes)**

Preheat the oven to 400°F or Mark 6 and then place a large griddle or frying pan on the hob over a high heat. Divide the chicken pieces onto each skewer, drizzle with olive oil and season well. Place the chicken skewers in the pre-heated griddle pan and cook for a few minutes until golden on each side. Meanwhile, blend all the remaining ingredients together to make the sauce. Remove the chicken skewers to a roasting pan and pour the piri piri sauce over the chicken and cook in oven for 30 minutes until cooked. Serve with a watercress salad. Serves 4.

The Crown Inn, Groombridge, Kent

Prawn Cocktail

1 lb. bag frozen large prawns   1 cos lettuce   Handful rocket leaves
1 avocado   Pinch cayenne pepper   1 lime, divided into 6 wedge-shaped sections

FOR THE SAUCE:
1 small jar mayonnaise   1 splash Worcestershire sauce
A few drops tabasco sauce   A dollop tomato ketchup
1 dessertspoon lime juice

Defrost the prawns in a colander at room temperature for around an hour. Scoop the mayonnaise into a bowl and add the remaining sauce ingredients. Stir and season to taste. Shred the lettuce and rocket and divide between 6 stemmed glasses, then peel and chop the avocado into small dice and scatter in each glass, mixing with the lettuce. Top with the prawns (retain 6 for decoration) and then the sauce. Garnish with a sprinkle of cayenne pepper, a wedge of lime and 1 prawn per glass. Serve with brown bread and butter. Serves 6.

Loaded Potato Skins

4 baking potatoes (large)   3 oz. mature cheddar or red Leicester (grated)
3 fl.oz. sour cream   2 spring onions (diced)   Pinch sea salt   Black pepper
1 tbsp. Worcestershire sauce   4 rashers streaky bacon   Oil (for frying)

Preheat the oven to 400°F or Mark 6 and bake the potatoes for around 1½ hours until cooked through. Cool slightly and then cut the potatoes lengthways and scoop the insides into a bowl. Put the skins of the potatoes to one side. Add half the grated cheese, spring onions and sour cream to the potato, mix well and season with salt and pepper and the Worcestershire sauce. Spoon the potato mixture into the potato skins and lay each half on a baking tray. Sprinkle over the remaining cheese and return to the oven to bake for 30 minutes until golden. Meanwhile, fry the bacon rashers in the oil until crispy, then shred and sprinkle over each cooked potato skin. Serve with a tomato salsa. Serves 4.

Cheesy Garlic Bread

**4 cloves garlic (crushed)   3½ oz. butter (softened)   1¾ oz. cheddar cheese (grated)
1 small red onion   1 baguette   2 tomatoes   Pinch mixed herbs**

Cream the softened butter and stir in the garlic, then add the herbs and grated cheese. Cut slits 2 inches apart along the length of a baguette and spread the garlic butter into both sides of the slits. Place the baguette on a piece of foil and wrap loosely. Bake at 400°F or Gas 6 for 10 minutes. Meanwhile, chop the tomatoes and onion finely and sprinkle over the cooked garlic bread as you are about to serve. Serves 4.

Carrot and Coriander Soup

**1 onion (chopped)   1 tsp. ground coriander   2 potatoes (chopped)   Oil (for frying)
1 lb. carrots (peeled and chopped)   2½ pints vegetable stock   Handful fresh coriander**

Heat the oil in a large pan, add the onion and sauté for around 5 minutes until tender. Stir in the ground coriander and potato, then cook for 1 minute. Add the carrots and stock, stir and bring to the boil. Reduce the heat, cover and simmer for 20 minutes until the carrots are tender. Cool and then pour into food processor with the fresh coriander and blitz until smooth. Return to pan, season and reheat to serve with chunks of crusty bread. Serves 4.

Liver Paté

6 oz. unsalted butter (softened)	2 cloves garlic (finely chopped)
1 lb. chicken livers	2 tbsp. brandy
2 shallots (finely chopped)	2 tsp. anchovy essence
1 tsp. thyme leaves (chopped)	Pinch ground black pepper

Butter (for frying)

Heat a knob of butter in a frying pan until foaming. Add the liver and fry for around 8 minutes, or until golden brown and cooked through. Then place the livers and pan juices in a food processor. In the same pan heat another knob of butter, add the shallots, thyme and garlic and sauté for around 5 minutes until the shallots are tender but not coloured. Add the brandy, anchovy essence and pepper and heat through. Place the shallot mixture in the food processor with the liver and add a further knob of butter, then blend until smooth. Place the paté in a serving dish, cover with cling film and refrigerate. Use within 48 hours. Serve with crusty bread and a sweet pickle on a bed of watercress. Serves 4.

The Bell Inn, Salford Priors, Worcestershire

Baked Camembert and Cranberry Chutney

BAKED CAMEMBERT:
**1 boxed Camembert cheese (in a wooden box) 2 sprigs thyme (leaves only)
1 tbsp. olive oil Sea salt and black pepper**

CRANBERRY CHUTNEY:
1 orange 3½ oz. cranberries 1¾ oz. light muscovado sugar 3 tbsp. port

Preheat the oven to 425°F or Mark 7. Unwrap the cheese and carefully slice the rind off the top of the cheese. Return the cheese to its box, cut-side up, and place the box on a baking sheet. Season the Camembert with sea salt and freshly ground pepper. Sprinkle over the thyme leaves and drizzle with olive oil. Bake for 10-15 minutes until the cheese is browned on top and melted inside. Allow to cool slightly, then serve with crusty bread and cranberry chutney. Serves 4.

Squeeze the orange and put the juice in a pan with the cranberries, sugar and port. Simmer for around 10 minutes until the cranberries start to soften and burst. Cool and place in a serving dish before chilling in the fridge. Serve with the baked Camembert.

Seasoned Potato Wedges

2 large potatoes (unpeeled)   Olive oil   Sea salt
Jars of seasoning – dried chillies, garlic, oregano, mixed herbs or Italian seasoning.

Preheat the oven to 425°F or Gas 7. Cut the potatoes into small wedges and place in a bowl. Drizzle over a little oil then sprinkle your choice of seasoning over the wedges. Toss well and add salt and pepper to taste. Oil a baking tray and spread the wedges evenly. Bake for around 20 minutes until golden brown and flip once halfway through. Serve with some homemade coleslaw. Serves 4 as a starter.

Deep Fried Garlic Mushrooms

10 fl.oz. soured cream   Pinch mixed herbs   1 garlic (crushed)
(seasoned to taste)   1 lb. small button mushrooms
2 tbsp. plain flour   2 medium eggs (beaten)
6 oz. brown breadcrumbs (seasoned with dried herbs)   Oil for deep frying

Combine the soured cream, crushed garlic and a pinch of mixed herbs to form the dip and refrigerate. Toss the mushrooms in the flour followed by the beaten egg, then coat with the breadcrumb mixture. Deep fry the mushrooms in hot oil for 5 minutes or until golden. Drain on kitchen paper and serve hot, accompanied by the dip. Serves 4.

The Old Boar's Head, Bishop's Stortford, Hertfordshire

Beer Battered Fish and Chips

FOR THE FISH:
1¾ oz. plain flour   1¾ oz. corn flour   1 tsp. baking powder   2½ fl.oz. ale
2½ fl.oz. sparkling water   2 pints sunflower oil (for frying)   2 x 8 oz. cod fillets

FOR THE CHIPS:
1½ lb. potatoes peeled and sliced into thick chips   2 tbsp. sunflower oil

Tip both the plain and corn flour and baking powder into a large bowl, then slowly whisk in the ale and sparkling water. Cut the potatoes into chunky chips and place them in a bowl of cold water until required. Drain and dry well before cooking. Heat the oil in a deep fat fryer to 280°F. Lower the chips into the hot fat, keeping the temperature at 280°F, and blanch them until the chips are soft but not coloured. Remove and leave on kitchen paper to drain and cool. Next, dust the fish fillets in a little plain flour, then dunk them into the batter, allowing any excess to drip off. Raise the temperature of the oil to 350°F or Mark 4, place the battered fish in the hot fat and fry for about 5 minutes or until golden brown. Remove, drain on kitchen paper and keep warm. Raise the temperature of the fat to 400°F or Mark 6, then return the blanched chips to the fryer and fry for several minutes until golden brown. Drain on kitchen paper, then serve the fish and chips with homemade mushy peas, tartar sauce and lemon halves. Serves 2.

Grilled Salmon with a Homemade Hollandaise Sauce

4 salmon fillets   3 eggs (separated)
5 oz. unsalted butter (cut into small chunks – room temperature)
1 lemon   Pinch of salt

To make the hollandaise sauce, squeeze a tablespoonful of lemon juice into a small saucepan. Add the yolks from the three eggs together with a knob of the butter and stir together with a wooden spoon. Add water to a larger saucepan and place a small heatproof glass bowl inside resting on an upturned saucer. Heat until the water just simmers, then stir in the butter, lemon and egg mixture for a couple of minutes before adding the remaining butter pieces. Stir gently until the sauce is smooth and thickened. Season to taste with salt and lemon juice. Take the bowl out of the saucepan and keep warm, stirring occasionally until the salmon has been grilled. Lay the salmon steaks on some foil and grill on both sides for around 5 minutes until cooked through. Serve covered with the hollandaise sauce and with buttered new potatoes and minted peas. Serves 4.

Grilled Steak and Chips

Rib-eye: allow 7-9 oz. per head to allow for trimming.
Cook with the surrounding fat still attached as the fat adds flavour as well as basting the meat during cooking, then trim as required before you serve.

Fillet: allow 3½ - 4½ oz. per head. It is very lean and tender, so no trimming of fat is required before or after cooking.

T-bone: allow 12-14 oz. per head, including the bone. Leave the fat on for cooking and trim as required before you serve.

To cook the steaks, heat a frying pan to a moderate heat for fillet, hot for T-bone or very hot for rib-eye. Add a little oil and a knob of butter, season the steaks with salt and pepper and cook for 1½-2½ minutes on each side for medium rare, depending on thickness of the meat. For fillet steak, cook the rounded edges too, turning to seal them well. Remove the steaks to a plate and allow resting for at least 5 minutes before you serve. Serve with your chosen sauce, homemade chunky chips, peas and a selection of side dishes including mushrooms, battered onion rings and a grilled tomato.

Homemade Quiche

½ oz. butter   1 large onion (thinly sliced)   1 red pepper (chopped)   3 large eggs (beaten)
3 oz. broccoli (cut into small florets)   7½ fl.oz. semi-skimmed milk   3 tbsp. chives (finely chopped)
4½ oz. mushrooms (sliced)   1 small can sweet corn (drained)   Salt and pepper   Oil
PASTRY: 4½ oz. plain flour   4½ oz. wholemeal flour   Pinch of cayenne pepper
4½ oz. butter (chilled and diced)   A little water (cold)

Sift both flours and the cayenne pepper into a bowl, rub in the butter until the mixture resembles fine crumbs. Sprinkle with 2 tbsp. of water and mix to a dough, adding extra water if required. Gather the dough into a ball, then roll out into an 11 inch circle about ⅛ inch thick. Line a loose-bottomed 9 inch fluted flan tin with the pastry, prick all over with a fork. Cover and chill for 30 minutes. Preheat oven to 400°F or Gas 6. Melt butter and a little oil in a frying pan and sauté the onion for 5 minutes. Blanch the red pepper in boiling water for 1 minute, then remove and drain. Add broccoli to the same water and blanch for 30 seconds, then remove and drain. Line the pastry case with greaseproof paper and cover with baking beans. Bake in the oven for 20 minutes. Remove the paper and beans and continue baking the pastry case for 5 minutes. Brush bottom of the pastry case with a little of the beaten egg and bake for 2 minutes. Remove from oven and reduce to 375°F or Gas 5. Beat the milk with the eggs, add the chives and seasoning to taste. Spread the onions in the pastry case, then add the red pepper, broccoli, mushrooms and sweet corn. Pour the egg mixture over the vegetables. Place quiche in the oven and bake for 40 minutes or until set. Leave to cool for at least 10 minutes. Serve warm.

Sixteen

The New Inn, Gloucester

Welsh Sausage and Mash with Burnt Leek Gravy

8 pork and leek sausages   2 leeks (cut finely)
6 large potatoes (peeled and quartered)
Splash milk or cream   Knob of butter
3½ oz. Caerphilly cheese (crumbled)
Peas and gravy (to serve)

Place the potatoes into a saucepan of water, bring to the boil and simmer for around 20 minutes or until tender. At the same time, fry the sausages for 20 minutes until brown and cooked through, adding the leeks for the final 10 minutes (ensuring leeks cook in the sausage fat but remain to one side of the pan). Remove the leeks when brown and drain on kitchen towel. Drain the potatoes then add a splash of milk or cream and a knob of butter and mash. Next, fold in the cheese and half the leeks to the mash and mix well. Make the gravy and add the remaining leeks, stir well. Serve with the sausages, mash, peas and gravy. Serves 4.

Yorkshire Puddings with Minced Beef and Horseradish

FOR THE YORKSHIRE PUDDING:
1 onion (finely chopped)   4 oz. plain flour   Pinch salt   1 egg
½ pint semi-skimmed milk   ½ tsp. mustard powder   Oil (for cooking)

FOR THE FILLING:
2 onions (chopped)   1 lb. minced beef   ¾ pint beef stock (made from a stock cube)
2 carrots (grated)   Handful frozen peas   Worcestershire sauce (a good shake)
4 tsp. horseradish sauce   Salt and white pepper (to taste)   Oil (for cooking)

To make the Yorkshire pudding, preheat the oven to 425°F or Gas 7. Sift the flour, mustard powder and a pinch of salt into a bowl. Beat the egg and milk to a smooth batter. Put a little oil and the chopped onion in a large round flan-type tin (not with a loose base), or individual smaller Yorkshire pudding tins and place in the oven for a few minutes until smoking hot. Pour the batter into the tin(s) and bake for around 40 minutes (30 minutes for smaller ones) until golden brown and well risen. Meanwhile, chop the remaining onions and sauté for 5 minutes. Add the minced beef and brown before stirring in the stock. Simmer for about 10 minutes. Add the grated carrot, peas, horseradish and Worcestershire sauce and simmer for 30 minutes. Season to taste. Fill the Yorkshire puddings with the minced beef and serve with crusty bread. Serves 4.

The Castle Inn, West Lulworth, Dorset

Coastal Fish Pie

1 lb. skinless fish (a mixture of smoked haddock, cod and salmon)
3½ oz. prawns (ready cooked, frozen)   9 fl.oz. full-fat milk   1 bay leaf
1 small onion (chopped)   2 eggs (hard boiled and sliced)   Small bunch parsley (chopped)
1¾ oz. butter   1 oz. plain flour   Pinch freshly grated nutmeg
1 lb. potato   1 oz. Cheddar cheese (grated)   Salt and pepper

Place the fish, onion and bay leaf in a large pan and pour over the milk. Bring to the boil and simmer gently for around 10 minutes. Lift the fish onto a plate and strain the milk into a jug to cool. Flake the fish into large pieces into the baking dish, add the cooked prawns and top with the slices of egg and a sprinkle of chopped parsley. Next, melt half the butter in a saucepan, stir in the flour and cook for 1 minute. Stir in the poached milk (save a little for the mashed potato) a little at a time, until the sauce is smooth. Simmer for 5 minutes, stirring all the time, then remove from the heat, season with salt, pepper and nutmeg and pour over the fish mixture. Meanwhile, preheat the oven to 400°F or Gas 6. Boil the potatoes for 20 minutes, then drain, season and mash with the remaining butter and the remaining poached milk. Top the pie with the mashed potato and fluff the top with a fork. Sprinkle with the cheese and bake for 40 minutes, or until the potato is golden brown and the sauce bubbling through. Serve with green beans and a grilled tomato. Serves 4.

Beef and English Ale Pie

2 lb. stewing beef (diced)	Pinch dried herbs
1 oz. flour (seasoned)	1 bay leaf
2 onions (chopped)	13½ fl.oz. ale
2 carrots (chopped)	1 pint beef stock
5 oz. button mushrooms	1 whole egg beaten with 1 egg yolk

10½ oz. ready-made rolled puff pastry

Dip the meat into the seasoned flour, then fry in a little oil, brown in a large frying pan for a few minutes until brown on all sides and set aside. Add the onions to the pan and sauté for 5 minutes until tender. Add the browned meat, vegetables and herbs to the onions, then pour in the ale and stock. Bring to a boil, cover and simmer gently on the hob for 1½ hours until tender. Preheat the oven to 425°F or Gas 7. Place the stew into an ovenproof pie dish and brush the edge with beaten egg. Roll out the puff pastry and place over the dish. Pinch the edges of the dish and trim any remaining pastry from around the edge. Decorate the top of the pie with any leftover pastry and then brush with the remaining beaten egg. Bake in the oven for 30 minutes until the pastry is golden brown. Serve with mashed potato and green beans. Serves 4.

Chicken Tikka Masala and Rice

½ oz. butter   2 onions (chopped)   3 tbsp. chicken tikka masala paste
1 red pepper (deseeded and cut into chunks)   4 chicken breasts (cubed)
1 x 14 oz. can chopped tomatoes   2 tbsp. tomato purée
2 tbsp. mango chutney   3 fl.oz. water   2½ fl.oz. double cream
2½ fl.oz. natural yogurt   Handful chopped coriander leaves, to serve
Oil (for frying)

Heat the oil and butter in a large, lidded casserole on the hob, then add the onions and sauté for 5 minutes until tender. Add the curry paste and peppers, then cook for 5 minutes, stirring to avoid any burning. Add the chicken pieces and stir well to coat in the paste. Cook for 5 minutes to seal the chicken, then add the tinned tomatoes, purée and water. Stir well, then cover with a lid and gently simmer for 20 minutes, stirring occasionally, until the chicken is cooked through. Remove the lid, stir in the mango chutney, cream and yogurt, then gently warm through. Serve with scattered coriander leaves, Basmati rice and warm naan bread. Serves 4.

Venison Casserole with Redcurrants

Knob of butter   2 onions (chopped)   2 garlic cloves (chopped)
2 rashers smoked bacon   8 oz. mushrooms   9 oz. shoulder of venison (diced)
½ bottle red wine   6 fl.oz. water   1 beef stock cube (crumbled)
2 tbsp. redcurrant jelly   Salt and black pepper
1 oz. corn flour (mixed with a little water)
1 small punnet redcurrants   Oil (for frying)

Preheat the oven to 300°F or Gas 2. On the hob, heat the olive oil and a knob of butter in a large lidded casserole dish. Add the onions and sauté for around 5 minutes until tender. Add the garlic, bacon and mushrooms and cook for a further minute or two. In a separate frying pan, brown the venison in batches and add to the casserole. Next, add the red wine, water, stock cube, redcurrant jelly and salt and pepper to taste. Bring to the boil and stir well. Put the lid on the casserole and place in the middle of the oven and cook for 90 minutes. Remove from the oven and add the corn flour paste, stirring well. Transfer the casserole to the hob and cook for a further 10 minutes over a low heat until the gravy has thickened. Serve with new potatoes and broccoli and decorate each plate with a bunch of fresh redcurrants. Serves 6.

The Cat and Fiddle Inn, New Forest, Hampshire

Beef Hotpot

2¼ lb. stewing beef (cubed)   1 can chopped tomatoes
3 oz. flour (seasoned)   12 fl.oz. beef stock
2 onions (chopped)   2 tsp dried mixed herbs
4 carrots (sliced)   Oil (for frying)

Coat the cubed beef in the seasoned flour and then brown in batches over a medium heat in a casserole for around 5 minutes. Remove the beef and add the onions and sauté for 5 minutes until tender. Add the carrots to the onions and cook for a further 2 minutes before adding the stock, tomatoes and dried herbs and heat through for a further few minutes. Next, return the beef to the pan, cover and bring to the boil, then simmer gently for 1½ hours. Serve piping hot with a baked potato and crusty bread.. Serves 6.

Chicken and Chorizo Casserole

4 chicken breasts (cubed)   7 oz. chorizo sausage (sliced)
1 onion (chopped)   4 garlic cloves (crushed)   2 celery sticks (sliced)
1 butternut squash (cubed)   6 fl.oz. white wine   1¼ pints chicken stock
1 can chopped tomatoes   Pinch dried herbs
1 tsp. paprika (smoked paprika works best)
Salt and pepper   Oil (for frying)

Preheat the oven to 350°F or Gas 4. Heat the oil in a casserole and cook the chicken and chorizo sausage until sealed all round. Remove and add the onion, garlic, celery and butternut squash and sauté gently for 20 minutes, stirring all the time. Add the wine, stock, chopped tomatoes, herbs, paprika and seasoning and heat through for a few minutes. Return the chicken and chorizo to the casserole, cover and cook in the oven for around 1 hour. Serve with chunks of Italian olive bread. Serves 4.

The White Hart Inn, Wytham, Oxfordshire

Vegetable Lasagne

1 aubergine (thinly sliced)   2 garlic cloves (crushed)   2 onions (chopped)
1 red and 1 green pepper (chopped)   8 oz. mushrooms (sliced)   2 celery sticks (sliced)
2 courgettes (cubed)   1 tsp. dried chilli pepper   2 cans chopped tomatoes
6 fl.oz. passata   1 pack lasagne sheets (no pre-cook variety)
Salt and pepper   Cheese sauce (made from 12 fl.oz. milk)
1 oz. cheese (grated)   Oil for frying

Preheat the oven to 350°F or Gas 4. Heat the oil in a large frying pan and cook the aubergine until brown on each side. Set aside on kitchen paper to drain. Add the onions to the hot oil and sauté for around 5 minutes until tender. Next, add the garlic, peppers, mushrooms, celery and courgettes and cook gently for 5 minutes, stirring all the time. Stir in the chilli powder and cook through for a minute or so and then add the chopped tomatoes, passata and a little seasoning. Cook through for a few further minutes. Place a layer of lasagne sheets in an ovenproof dish and top with a few spoons of the vegetable mixture and sliced aubergine. Next, drizzle over some cheese sauce and continue these layers 2 more times, finishing with cheese sauce on the top. Sprinkle with the grated cheese and place in the oven for 40 minutes or until golden brown. Serve with a crisp green salad. Serves 6.

Ploughman's Lunch

FOR EACH SERVING:
Selection of local cheeses (cut into chunks)   1 slice of ham or a slice of pork pie
1 tomato (quartered)   1 celery stick   1 handful of cos lettuce (shredded)
1 scoop of coleslaw   Pickled onions   Dollop of pickles
Small bunch of seedless grapes   Chunk of crusty bread

Arrange the colourful ingredients on a plate and serve in your own garden with cool and refreshing elderberry fizz.

Elderberry Fizz

FOR EACH SERVING:
1 part elderberry cordial   4 parts fizzy rose wine

Mix and enjoy in your very own garden with a tasty ploughman's lunch.

Chop House Mixed Grill

4 lamb chops   4 Lamb kidneys (skinned, halved and cored)
4 small steaks   4 small gammon steaks   4 pork sausages
Knob of butter (melted)   Salt and black pepper (to taste)
4 large tomatoes   4 large mushrooms   Handful watercress
Jar English mustard (to serve)

Prepare a BBQ grill, or preheat a cooker grill to its hottest. Brush the chops, kidney halves and steaks with the melted butter and season with salt and pepper. Place the chops, kidneys, sausages and gammon on the grill and cook for about 5-7 minutes each side, depending on their thickness. Next, add the steaks, allowing 3 minutes per side for medium rare. Remove the meat and keep warm (covered in a warm oven is best). Brush the tomatoes and mushrooms with melted butter and grill for about 5 minutes. Arrange the meat, tomatoes and mushrooms on warmed plates and garnish with the watercress just before you serve, together with a dollop of English mustard. Serves 4.

Warm Chocolate Fudge Cake with Ice Cream

FOR THE SPONGE:

**3 oz. self-raising flour   1 oz. cocoa powder   4 oz. light muscovado sugar
4 oz. unsalted butter (softened)   1 tsp. vanilla essence
2 free-range eggs (lightly beaten)   3 tbsp. milk   Pinch of salt**

FOR THE SAUCE:

3 oz. light muscovado sugar   1 oz. cocoa powder   ½ pint milk

Preheat the oven to 350°F or Gas 4. First, make the sponge by sifting the flour into a bowl with the cocoa powder and salt. In a separate bowl, cream together the sugar and butter until light and fluffy. Beat in the vanilla essence and the eggs, then fold this mixture in the flour mixture. Mix in just enough milk to give a soft dropping consistency, then spoon into a buttered 2 pint ovenproof dish.   For the sauce, mix the sugar and the cocoa powder together and gradually beat in the milk. Pour evenly over the uncooked cake mixture and place in the oven and bake for around 60 minutes until the cake is firm and spongy to touch. Serve hot with a scoop of vanilla ice cream. Serves 4.

The Bell Inn, Waltham St. Lawrence, Berkshire

Chocolate Sundae

FOR THE SUNDAE:
1 tub (18 fl.oz.) vanilla ice cream (you will not use all)
1 pack (5 oz.) shortbread biscuits (broken into small pieces)
4 small slices of chocolate cake (chopped into bite-size pieces).
3½ oz. dark chocolate (chopped)   10 fresh strawberries (chopped)

FOR THE SAUCE:
7 oz. milk chocolate   ½ oz. butter   4 oz. icing sugar
3½ fl.oz. single cream   2 tbs. golden syrup

First, to make the sauce, gently melt the milk chocolate with the butter in a bowl over boiling water and stir until there are no lumps. Remove from the heat and leave to cool for 5 minutes and then fold in the cream. Sift in the icing sugar and stir. Put the sauce into a heavy-based saucepan and add the golden syrup. Gently heat through for a few minutes until the sauce is pourable.

For the sundae, layer the ingredients into individual sundae glasses and then pour the warm sauce over the top and finish off with some remaining strawberries. Serve warm.

Knickerbocker Glory

4 strawberries
Bottle of strawberry sauce
Ice cream (try unusual flavours)
1 jar strawberry jam (good quality)
3 fl.oz. double cream (whipped to soft peak consistency)
2 flake chocolate bars (broken in half)
4 glacé cherries

Place a strawberry at the bottom of each knickerbocker glass and squirt a little strawberry sauce around it. Then add a scoop of ice cream, topped with a dollop of strawberry jam. Repeat this process with more layers, finishing with ice cream. Next, pipe the cream over the top of the ice cream and finish with a final squirt of strawberry sauce, half a flake and a glacé cherry. Serve immediately. Serves 4.

The Crab Inn, Shanklin Old Village, Isle of Wight

Banoffee Pie

10½ oz. oaty-type biscuits (Hob Nobs)   2½ oz. butter (melted)
14 oz. tin caramel (ready prepared)   4 bananas (sliced)
12 fl.oz. double cream   1 tbsp. icing sugar
3½ oz. dark chocolate

Preheat the oven to 350°F or Gas 4. Crush the biscuits in a food processor then add the melted butter and pulse to combine. Press the biscuit mixture into a 9 in. tart tin, with a removable base, in an even layer. Cook in the oven for around 20 minutes, until lightly toasted and set. Leave to cool, then gently release from the tin and put on a serving plate.

Spread the caramel over the biscuit base and chill for 1 hour, then arrange the banana slices over the caramel. Whip the cream and sugar together to form soft peaks and spread over the bananas. Melt the chocolate in a bowl set over a pan of simmering water. Allow to cool slightly, before drizzling over the cream.

Serve chilled with an extra dollop of whipped cream. Serves 4.

Kentish Apple Pie and Custard

FOR THE PASTRY:
9 oz. plain flour   Pinch of salt   5 oz. hard margarine
6 tsp. cold water   Demerara sugar (for sprinkling)

FOR THE FILLING:
4 Bramley cooking apples (chopped, stewed and cooled)   1 tsp. sugar

Preheat the oven to 400F° or Gas 6. Sieve the flour and salt into a bowl. Rub in the margarine until the mixture resembles fine breadcrumbs. Add the cold water to the flour mixture and mix to form a pastry dough. Divide the pastry into two halves. Roll one half so that it is big enough to cover an 8 inch pie plate. Fill the pastry with the stewed apples and sprinkle with sugar to taste. Roll out the other half of the pastry, moisten the edge of the bottom layer of pastry and place the second piece on top. Press down and seal the pastry edges. Trim off any excess pastry with a knife and flute the edges. Prick the surface of the pastry and sprinkle with demerara sugar before placing the pie in the oven. Cook for 30 minutes until golden brown.

Serve with lashings of thick custard. Serves 6.

Vegetarian Chilli

**1 small can sweet corn   1 large onion, chopped   2 cloves garlic, crushed
2 tsp. chilli powder   1 tsp. cumin seeds   1 aubergine (sliced)
1 red and 1 green pepper (chopped)   2 carrots, peeled and chopped
2 x 14 oz. cans chopped tomatoes   1 14 oz. can mixed beans (drained)
2 tbsp. tomato purée   10 fl.oz. vegetable stock   3½ oz. frozen peas
6 oz. mushrooms (chopped)   1 courgette (chopped)
Salt and black pepper (pinch of each)
Oil (for frying)**

Heat the oil in a large saucepan and fry the sliced aubergine until brown on each side and set aside on kitchen paper. Then sauté the onion and garlic together with the chilli and cumin for around 10 minutes until the onions are soft. Add the peppers and carrots and cook for 5 minutes, stirring all the time. Add the chopped tomatoes, tomato purée, stock and peas, bring to the boil and simmer for about 30 minutes. Add the mushrooms, sweet corn and courgettes and simmer for 5 minutes more. Add the mixed beans and simmer for 5 more minutes. Serve with cooked rice or jacket potato. Serves 4.

Scampi and Chips

FOR THE SCAMPI:
2 eggs (separated)   5 oz. plain flour   Salt and black pepper (pinch of each)
8½ fl.oz. bottled ale   14 oz. monkfish fillets

FOR THE HOMEMADE TARTAR SAUCE:
2 large egg yolks   1 tsp. white wine vinegar   ½ tsp. mustard powder   1 tsp. salt
1 lemon, juice only   9 fl.oz. rapeseed oil   2 tbsp. chopped capers
4 gherkins, chopped   1 tbsp. parsley

For the 'scampi', place the egg yolks, flour, salt and black pepper in a bowl and whisk together. Add the beer and whisk to a smooth batter. Place the egg whites into a separate bowl and whisk until stiff peaks form. Add half of the egg whites to the batter and mix well, then carefully fold in the remaining egg whites. Dip the monkfish chunks into the batter then place them in a deep fat fryer at 375°F and cook for around 3 minutes until golden brown. Remove from the oil and drain on kitchen paper. For the tartar sauce, place the egg yolks, vinegar, mustard, salt and lemon juice into a food processor and blend well. Then gradually add the rapeseed oil and blend until the sauce has thickened. Spoon the mixture into a bowl, add the remaining ingredients and mix well. Season to taste with salt and freshly ground black pepper. To serve, place equal amounts of the fried monkfish and chips onto each plate and serve with a dollop of tartar sauce alongside.

Ye Olde King's Head, Chigwell, Essex

Smoked Haddock Fish Cakes

**6 medium potatoes (cubed)   8½ fl.oz. milk
2 salmon fillets   2 smoked haddock fillets
7 oz. king prawns (chopped)   Salt and pepper to taste
2 tbsp. mayonnaise   4 oz. plain flour
2 eggs   5 oz. breadcrumbs (or crushed cornflakes)**

Boil potatoes, drain, and then mash and set aside. Bring the milk to the boil, then reduce the heat, add the salmon and haddock fillets and simmer for 5 minutes. Remove the fish to a large bowl and fork into small pieces. Mix together the fish, prawns, mashed potatoes and mayonnaise, then season with a little salt and pepper. Whisk the eggs in shallow bowl, place the flour in another and the breadcrumbs in a third. Make 8 patties from the fish mixture, then cover in flour, dip in the egg and finally in the breadcrumbs.

Fry the fish cakes in a large frying pan for a few minutes each side until golden brown. Then place on a baking tray in a preheated oven at 400°F or Gas 6 for 10-15 minutes to cook through. Serve with homemade chunky chips. Serves 4.

Marie Rose Sandwich

8 slices white bread (buttered)
2 tbsp. mayonnaise
1 tbsp. tomato ketchup
Pinch of cayenne pepper

Pinch sea salt and black pepper
1 lemon (juice)
4 handfuls of cooked, peeled prawns
Cress (to garnish)

Add the mayonnaise, tomato ketchup and cayenne pepper to a bowl, season with a pinch of salt and pepper and mix well. Squeeze the lemon juice into the bowl and then fold in the prawns until they are well coated. Use as a filling to make your sandwiches, then cut the bread diagonally and sprinkle with cress before you serve. Serves 4.

The Barley Mow, Clifton Hampden, Oxfordshire

Jacket Potato and Coronation Chicken

2 chicken breast fillets (cooked and diced)   4 large baking potatoes
1 small stalk celery (chopped)   ½ small red onion (chopped)
1 small apple (peeled, cored and chopped)   ¾ oz. sultanas
¾ oz. seedless green grapes (halved)   ¾ oz. toasted pecans (chopped)
Pinch black pepper   Sea salt   ¼ tsp. curry powder
3 oz. mayonnaise   Olive oil   Cress (enough for a garnish)

In a large bowl, mix together all the ingredients apart from the chicken. Then add the chicken and toss until well coated. Cover and refrigerate until serving. Prick the potatoes and rub them over with a little olive oil and then sprinkle with salt. Place on a baking tray and cook in a hot oven (375°F or Gas 5) for 1 hour to 1 hour and 20 minutes (or until cooked). Slice open your potatoes and divide the Coronation chicken mixture between your potatoes. Sprinkle over the cress before serving. Serves 4.

Scottish Beef Burger with Stilton Cheese

1 lb. minced beef	1 tsp. prepared mustard
1 onion (finely chopped)	1¾ oz. crumbled stilton cheese
1 celery stick (chopped)	4 large burger buns
1 tsp. dried mixed herbs	Salt and black pepper

Place the minced beef in a bowl together with the onion, dried herbs, mustard and celery and season to taste. Form into a firm mixture with your hands and divide into 8 equal portions. Place 4 on a plate and flatten each one slightly, then divide the crumbled cheese in the centre of each. Next, flatten the remaining 4 portions and place on top. Next, mould each burger together encasing the crumbled cheese and shape. Grill under a medium heat for around 10 minutes each side until cooked through. Meanwhile, split the burger buns and place a burger inside each. Serve with salad and a dollop of thick tomato ketchup. Serves 4.

Grilled BBQ Chicken Melt Sandwich

4 portions chicken breast   2 onions (sliced)
8 tender asparagus sticks   4 burger rolls
4 slices Cheddar cheese   Salt and pepper (to taste)
Olive oil (for cooking)   BBQ sauce (squeezy bottle)

Lightly oil the asparagus and onion and season with salt and pepper. Place on the grill and cook under a low heat for around 5 minutes. Remove onion slices when they are starting to brown and remove the asparagus when it gets soft and set aside. Add the chicken portions and grill for around 10 minutes each side and until cooked through. Next, squeeze over the chicken a dollop BBQ sauce and grill for 1 further minute each side, adding another dollop of BBQ sauce when you turn. Meanwhile, toast the rolls on the outside only.

To serve, place the rolls on a baking sheet, toasted side down. Top with the chicken, asparagus, onion and then a cheese slice. Place under the grill for a few minutes to melt the cheese, then add a dollop of BBQ sauce and the top half of the bun. Serve with a green crispy salad. Serves 4.

METRIC CONVERSIONS

The weights, measures and oven temperatures used in the preceding recipes can be easily converted to their metric equivalents. The conversions listed below are only approximate, having been rounded up or down as may be appropriate.

Weights

Avoirdupois	Metric
1 oz.	just under 30 grams
4 oz. (¼ lb.)	app. 115 grams
8 oz. (½ lb.)	app. 230 grams
1 lb.	454 grams

Liquid Measures

Imperial	Metric
1 tablespoon (liquid only)	20 millilitres
1 fl. oz.	app. 30 millilitres
1 gill (¼ pt.)	app. 145 millilitres
½ pt.	app. 285 millilitres
1 pt.	app. 570 millilitres
1 qt.	app. 1.140 litres

Oven Temperatures

	°Fahrenheit	Gas Mark	°Celsius
Slow	300	2	150
	325	3	170
Moderate	350	4	180
	375	5	190
	400	6	200
Hot	425	7	220
	450	8	230
	475	9	240

Flour as specified in these recipes refers to plain flour unless otherwise described.